The Game of Mah Jong

The Game of
MAH JONG

Max Robertson

PENGUIN BOOKS

Published by the Penguin Group

Penguin Group (NZ), 67 Apollo Drive, Rosedale,
North Shore 0632, New Zealand (a division of Pearson New Zealand Ltd)
Penguin Group (USA) Inc., 375 Hudson Street,
New York, New York 10014, USA
Penguin Group (Canada), 90 Eglinton Avenue East, Suite 700, Toronto,
Ontario, M4P 2Y3, Canada (a division of Pearson Penguin Canada Inc.)
Penguin Books Ltd, 80 Strand, London, WC2R 0RL, England
Penguin Ireland, 25 St Stephen's Green,
Dublin 2, Ireland (a division of Penguin Books Ltd)
Penguin Group (Australia), 250 Camberwell Road, Camberwell,
Victoria 3124, Australia (a division of Pearson Australia Group Pty Ltd)
Penguin Books India Pvt Ltd, 11, Community Centre,
Panchsheel Park, New Delhi – 110 017, India
Penguin Books (South Africa) (Pty) Ltd, 24 Sturdee Avenue,
Rosebank, Johannesburg 2196, South Africa

Penguin Books Ltd, Registered Offices: 80 Strand, London, WC2R 0RL, England

First published by Whitcoulls Limited, 1974
This edition published by Penguin Group (NZ), 2007
20 19 18 17 16 15 14 13

Designed by Renee Greenland
Printed by Everbest Printing Co. Ltd, China

ISBN – 13: 978 014 300659 6

A catalogue record for this book is available from the National Library of New
Zealand.

www.penguin.co.nz

CONTENTS

PREFACE

In writing this book on the game of Mah Jong, difficulty was encountered in compiling rules and scoring to suit all players. It will be found that these rules will vary slightly in places, though the actual method of playing and types of hands have been practically adhered to.

It is a pity that Mah Jong players do not use one set of rules as this would avoid any risk of argument. A Chinese gentleman once remarked: "We Chinese have played Mah Jong one way for a thousand years, but you foreigners have played it a thousand ways in one year". However, if the rules and scoring in this book are closely followed players will be playing correctly and by the most up-to-date methods.

If all players would strictly adhere to this set of rules they would more or less become universal. Argument as to correct play would be avoided, more pleasure would be experienced in the playing, and confidence would be the keynote when contesting with strangers, as all possibility of differences would be eliminated. After all the game was invented by the Chinese and their rules should be followed as closely as possible.

A large volume could be compiled on the playing of Mah Jong, but as most people want to learn quickly this book has been written as simply as possible. It contains merely the necessary rules and scoring, with a selection of hands.

PART I

THE GAME OF MAH JONG

THE GAME OF MAH JONG

The game of Mah Jong was invented by the Chinese hundreds of years ago, and has been played throughout China down the centuries. It is only in recent years that it has spread to the Western World where it has taken on like wildfire.

The Western game varies somewhat form the old Chinese game, but the principles and scoring are exactly the same, the only difference being the types of hands plus a slight variation in the doubling.

The Chinese game (see page 91) is very simple and has no complicated hands as has the Western. More skill is required for the latter, though in some ways it is more obvious and easier to tell what type of hand another player is going for by his discards. The Chinese game, on the other hand, is far more mysterious.

When Mah Jong was introduced to the Western world the rules were altered and amended to make it more interesting and exciting and today the craze for this fascinating game has become almost universal.

To become proficient, Mah Jong players are advised to carefully study the rules in this book and go through them thoroughly, memorising every little point of play. It is only through careful study of these, together with plenty of practice and concentration, that a player can become an expert. At first the game seems most complicated – more so than Bridge – but actually, it is very easy once the rules have been mastered. When this is done and a player has learnt all there is to know about Mah Jong – the rest is luck.

Remember: concentration, patience and quickness of play, make the good player.

THE SET OF MAH JONG

There are many types of Mah Jong sets on the market, the most popular being the bone and bamboo backed tiles. These all vary in quality. Some sets have quarter-bone, half-bone, and three-bone faces dovetailed into the bamboo. There are also some very attractive sets with coloured backs in red, blue, orange, jade, black and amber, etc. A Mah Jong table can be made to look very pleasing to the eye by using a contrasting coloured material to cover the table, or a matching material of a paler or darker shade than the colour of the backs. The racks can also be lacquered to tone in with the colour scheme.

Players are advised when buying a Mah Jong set to see that all tiles are carefully and clearly marked with the English numerals and letters, especially the Character Suit, The Winds, and Flowers. If these titles are indistinct confusion will arise as to which is which.

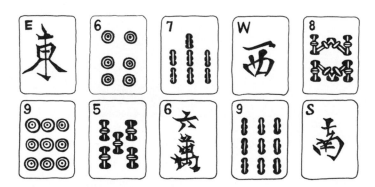

TILES

A Mah Jong set is made up of 144 pieces known as Tiles. These are divided into two sections:

(A) HONOUR TILES, and (B) SUIT TILES.

(A) HONOUR TILES. These tiles are:

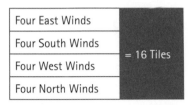

Four Red Dragons	
Four Green Dragons	= 12 Tiles
Four White Dragons	

Four East Winds	
Four South Winds	= 16 Tiles
Four West Winds	
Four North Winds	

> N.B Players should also note carefully that the 1's and 9's of each suit are also known as Honour Tiles.

(B) SUIT TILES. These tiles comprise three distinct sets – Bamboos, Circles, and Characters. The Tiles in each of these three suits are numbered from 1 to 9 inclusive, of which there are four of each. Therefore there are:

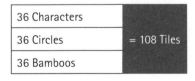

36 Characters	
36 Circles	= 108 Tiles
36 Bamboos	

This makes a total of 136 tiles. The balance of the 144 tiles, eight in all, are known as Flowers and Seasons. These do not enter into the actual play of the forming of a Mah Jong Hand. They merely affect the score and are dealt with later.

EXTRA TILES

In every Mah Jong set there are four extra plain white tiles, similar to the White Dragons. These are put in the set in case a tile is lost, when one of these extra tiles can be engraved to take the place of the lost tile. Players should be careful not to use these four extra tiles when playing the game, as they are the same as the White Dragons. It is advisable to take out the extra tiles from the set and put them away in a safe place.

COUNTERS AND DICE

In every Mah Jong set, there are four or six dice, of which only two are used, and a set of counters or chips used for paying the total scores of each player. This is explained more fully later.

RACKS

A set of wooden racks is required to place the tiles on during play. There are several different types to be had and these are left to the player's own choice. It is very convenient to have four small wooden drawers made to keep the counters in. These can be screwed on to an ordinary Bridge table so that they can be pushed under the table when not in use.

DOUBLING CARD

This is supplied at the back of this book and is a very convenient method of doubling a player's scores.

PART II

PRELIMINARY STAGES

PRELIMINARY STAGES

The game is played by three or four players, preferably four, although the three-handed Mah Jong is a very exciting and good game. Also two can play an interesting game. Both the three-handed and two-handed games are described later.

The players determine their seats by throwing in turn two dice, and adding the numbers shown on the dice together, the highest total having choice of seats. After this has been done players in turn again throw the dice, the highest total becomes East Wind. The player on East Wind's right is South Wind; the player on East Wind's left is North Wind and the player opposite East Wind is West Wind. It is important to note which player was first to be East Wind, as the Wind of the Round (explained later) changes when the original East Wind become East Wind again.

 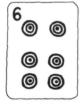 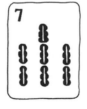  

After the Winds have been allocated, the next step is to shuffle the tiles, which is done with them face downwards. This shuffling is known as "The Twittering of The Sparrows". The players then proceed to build a square of four Walls, each of two rows of 18 tiles, one on top of the other, one Wall being built by each player. These four Walls must be pushed into the centre so that they touch the Walls on either side to "Keep the Devils Out". This square of tiles is known as "The Great Wall of China".

East Wind then throws the two dice to determine where the Wall is to be opened. He adds the total of the throw together and counts the four sides of the Square in an anticlockwise direction, beginning with his own Wall as No. 1. South would be No. 2, West No. 3, and so on. Thus if the dice result was five, East Wind's own Wall would be broken. 11 would be West Wind's, etc. When the Wall to be opened has been determined, the player whose Wall has to be opened, proceeds to count the number thrown from the right of his Wall, to ascertain where the Wall has to be opened. Therefore the one throw of the two dice not only determines which Wall has to be opened but also the actual place it has to be broken at.

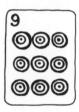 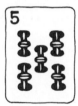  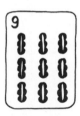 

E.g. East Wind threw the two dice, the total being 11. This means West Wind's Wall has to be broken at the 11th tile from the right of his Wall. When the two tiles to be removed are ascertained, the player lifts out these two tiles and places them on the second and seventh tiles to the right of the opening. These two tiles on top of the Wall are known as Loose Tiles (the use of these Loose Tiles is explained later).

East Wind then proceeds to draw four tiles from the left of the opening for his own hand, then the other players each in turn, in an anticlockwise direction, i.e., East, South, West and North draw four tiles, until all players have twelve tiles, when East

Wind takes the 1st and 3rd tiles from the top row of the Wall, the remaining three players each take one tile, in turn as before. It will be found that East Wind has now fourteen tiles, and each of the other players thirteen tiles. The next stage is to look for the Flower Tiles. These are placed on the table face downwards and a Loose Tile is taken from the Wall to replace it. This is done in rotation, commencing with East Wind in an anticlockwise direction. Should East Wind pick a Loose Tile for his Flower and this tile be another Flower, he takes another Loose Tile, **before the next player** takes his Loose Tile for his Flower. This applies to each player in turn. If later in the game a player picks up a Flower from the Wall, he proceeds in the same manner by turning it face downwards on the table and replacing it in his playing hand by a Loose Tile. The players now arrange their tiles into their various suits, placing two or three or four of the same tile together and forming any or part of a run of three together, and estimate what type of hand it would be best to try and obtain. This is done by picking a tile from the Wall and discarding a tile not wanted from the player's hand, and by Punging, Konging and Chowing from another player's discard (explained later).

East Wind is always the first to start the game by discarding a tile he does not require, face upwards on the table for the other players to see. This leaves him with thirteen tiles, the same as the other players, and then the actual play begins.

The object of the game is to obtain a complete Mah Jong Hand made up of **four sets and one Pair of tiles** known as Pung, Kong and Chow, or any of the special hands mentioned later.

PUNG, KONG, CHOW, PAIR

PUNG

(A) EXPOSED PUNG: Any three of a kind is called a Pung. This is obtained by forming a Pair (see page 24) concealed in the hand first, and a third tile to make the Pung is obtained from any other player's discarded tile immediately after the discard has been made. When a Pung has been formed in this manner the player announces "Pung" and places it face upwards on the table in front of him. This is known as an Exposed Pung and scores 2 points for Suit Tiles and 4 points for Honour Tiles.

(B) CONCEALED PUNG: Should a player, having obtained a pair concealed in the hand first, draw the third tile from the Wall himself, to make a Pung, he retains this Pung in his concealed hand and does not declare it face up on the table. This Pung is known as a Concealed Pung, and it is worth twice as much as an Exposed Pung, i.e. 4 points for a Suit Pung and 8 Points for an Honour Pung.

   This Concealed Pung is retained in the hand until one of the players announces Mah Jong. It is then placed on the table along with any of the other Pungs and Kongs. To show that this is a Concealed Pung, the middle tile of this Pung is turned face downwards.

KONG

Any four of a kind is known as a Kong, and is obtained by forming either an Exposed Pung or a Concealed Pung first.

(A) EXPOSED KONG:

Formed in two ways –

1. A player must have a Concealed Pung in his hand first and one of the other players discards the fourth of this kind. The player with the Concealed Pung may claim this discard immediately to form the Exposed Kong, announcing Kong. He places it face up on the table in front of him. This is known as an Exposed Kong.

2. A player must have an Exposed Pung declared on the table and he draws from the Wall himself, the fourth tile of this kind. He may then place this tile alongside the Exposed Pung, thereby forming an Exposed Kong.

   However, if any other player discards the fourth tile of any Exposed Pung, the player with this Exposed Pung cannot claim this tile to make his Pung into an Exposed Kong. He can only make an Exposed Pung into an Exposed Kong by drawing the fourth tile from the Wall himself.

   Exposed Kongs of Suit Tiles score 8 points and 16 points for Honour Tiles.

(B) CONCEALED KONG: A player must have a Concealed Pung already formed in his hand first. He then draws from the Wall himself the fourth tile of this kind, which forms a Concealed Kong. These Kongs score twice the value of Exposed Kongs, i.e. Concealed Kongs of Suit Tiles score 16 points and 32 points for Concealed Kongs of Honour Tiles.

SPECIAL RULES FOR KONGS

(1) EXPOSED KONGS: As soon as a player has made an Exposed Kong he declares it on the table in front of him, and then **draws one of the Loose Tiles from the Wall which he places in his concealed hand**. This is most important to remember.

(2) CONCEALED KONG: When a player has formed a Concealed Kong he at once declares it on the table in front of him and draws one of the Loose Tiles from the Wall, which he places in his concealed hand. It is most important to remember that a Concealed Kong must be declared on the table in the above manner, otherwise it can only be scored as a Concealed Pung, if retained in the hand. It is not necessary to declare a Kong immediately it is formed, except, of course, when made with a discarded tile. Even then a player may Pung it, retaining the fourth tile in his hand and Konging it at a later stage. This is often a better method, as a player may want one of the Kong Tiles to form a Chow, and once he has declared a Kong, he cannot use one of these tiles for a Chow. Remember, you can make a Pung first and Kong it later at any stage of the game, but only when it is the player's turn.

Though a Concealed Kong has been exposed, it still remains and scores as a Concealed Kong. To show that it is a Concealed Kong, the two middle tiles are turned face downwards to distinguish it from an Exposed Kong. No player can have a complete Mah Jong Hand with a Concealed Kong retained in the hand.

It must be noted, and this is very important, that a player who has gone Mah Jong may find he has to discard one of his four sets of tiles, a Kong, making a total number of fifteen tiles instead of fourteen – 2 Kongs would mean 16 tiles; 3 Kongs would mean 17 tiles. This is quite correct for the reason that when he made the

Kong, he took a Loose Tile from the Wall into his hand to make up for the extra tile he took from his hand to make the Kong. So that, during the playing of a game a player may count up his tiles to see if he has the correct number (13) and find instead he has 14, there being one Kong on the table in front of him. Always look upon a Kong as **one set of tiles** and count it as three tiles and not four, though it scores as four tiles.

Always remember that as soon as a player has declared a Kong on the table in front of him he **must take a Loose Tile and place it in his playing hand**, otherwise he will be one tile short and cannot go Mah Jong. So many players forget this point and wonder why they are a tile short, the reason being that they declare their Kong and discard a tile without taking a Loose Tile. This cannot be corrected, and the player has to continue playing with a tile short and cannot go Mah Jong.

CHOW

A sequence of three tiles only, all three in the same suit is known as a Chow, and is formed by Chowing a discarded tile immediately after it has been discarded, from the player on **the left** of the player who requires that tile to make the sequence.

Before a player can Chow a tile from the player on his left he must have **two other tiles concealed in his hand** forming part of the Chow. He cannot pick up a discarded tile to form part of the Chow, i.e. two tiles, but can only draw these two from the Wall himself. He can then complete the Chow by taking the third from the discard of the player on his left. He must then declare his Chow on the table in front of him.

However, should a player draw all three tiles for a Chow from the Wall himself, he retains this Chow concealed in his hand. All Chows have no scoring value and are merely used to help to complete the hand, therefore they are to be avoided if possible, for the reason that a completed hand which has no Chow in it scores one extra double i.e., an all Pung hand.

Should a player be waiting for one tile to complete his whole hand, and the tile required is one to form a Chow, he may take this tile from **any player's discard.**

Only one Chow is permitted in a complete Mah Jong Hand (except a Concealed Mah Jong, which is explained later).

A PAIR

Every completed Mah Jong Hand **must have one Pair in it**, this Pair being known as the Sparrows Head. No hand is complete without this Pair and there are **no exceptions** (all Pair Hands, of course, contain 7 Pairs).

Sometimes a player finds that he has completed the four sets of tiles and has one odd tile left. This means that he is waiting to complete his Pair to give him a full Mah Jong hand. He may claim a mate for this tile from any of the other player's discards unless he draws it from the Wall himself. This is the one exception when a discarded tile may be claimed to form a Pair, that is to complete a Mah Jong Hand.

Pairs, as a rule, have **no scoring value**, but there are times when they do score (see Chapter on Scoring), also Pairs are never entitled to a double.

LOOSE TILES

These tiles are very important to remember, as many a player finds himself during a game, one tile short, the reason being that he has forgotten to take a Loose Tile for his Kongs and Flowers.

The Loose Tiles are these which are placed on top of the Wall when it was first opened – this has been explained previously. As soon as any player makes a Kong and declares it on the table, he immediately takes one of the Loose Tiles and places it in his hand, and then discards a tile from his hand.

Also, when a player draws a Flower or Season from the Wall and places this Tile face downwards on the table in front of him (see Flowers and Seasons), he takes one of these Loose Tiles and places it in his hand and discards a tile not required. If he should draw a Flower when it is a Loose Tile he proceeds in the same manner by drawing another Loose Tile and then discarding.

As soon as the two Loose Tiles have been used up, two more from that end of the Wall are placed on top of the Wall to replace the two used, and so on. If a player draws a Loose Tile and it completes his hand for Mah Jong, he doubles his total score once.

Beginners are often a little confused over these Loose Tiles, when they are approaching the last few Tiles of the Wall to be drawn for their turns. In this case the Loose Tiles are replaced to their original position at the end of the Wall and are drawn eventually for a player's turn. If a Kong is made or a Flower drawn when the Wall is almost finished and the Loose Tiles have been replaced as above, the player just takes one of the tiles which has been replaced at the end of the Wall.

DEAD TILES

As soon as a player discards a tile it may be claimed by any other player to form a Pung, Kong or Chow (from the player on the discarder's right only), or to complete a Mah Jong Hand, but this must be done **immediately the discard is made and before the next player in turn discards**. If no player wants this discarded tile it becomes what is known as a Dead Tile and takes no further part in the play of that game. Thus it cannot be claimed at a later stage of the game.

Players are advised to carefully watch all these Dead Tiles as they may find themselves waiting for a tile to make a Pung with perhaps two or three of them already discarded.

FLOWERS

In every set of Mah Jong there are eight tiles called Flowers and Seasons. To distinguish the Flowers from the Seasons is very difficult, so to simplify matters they are all known as Flowers. These Flowers actually take no part in the play of the hand – they are merely added to the set as an extra and affect the score only.

These Flowers are divided into two sets of four tiles, numbered from one to four, inclusive, one set being numbered with red figures, and one with blue, green or black, according to the sets. In some sets four of these Flowers are marked N.S.E.W. to distinguish them from the other set.

As explained previously, as soon as a player draws a Flower from the Wall he places it **face downwards** in front of him to conceal it and replaces it in his hand by drawing a Loose Tile and then discarding a tile.

Should a player eventually draw a complete set of four tiles – numbers 1 to 4, all of the same colour – he has what is known as a Bouquet.

For every Flower drawn by a player he adds 4 points extra to his score and doubles his total score once extra for each of his own Flowers, No. 1 being East Wind's own Flower, No. 2 being South Wind's, No. 3 being West Wind's, and No. 4 being North Wind's. Of course the Flowers marked N.S.E.W. correspond with the player's own Wind.

Should a player form a Bouquet, he doubles his total score three times extra (these three doubles include the one double for the owner's Flower contained in the Bouquet) and takes another double as well if he has his own Flower from the other set.

N.B. Among some players there exists a rule whereby a player may double his score if he has the Flower of the Wind of the Round (explained later). This rule is not strictly correct according to the Chinese rules, but may be used. This must be settled before the game commences.

LOOSE TILES OR JOKERS

When a player has an Exposed Kong of tiles in which is included a Loose Tile, should he then pick up from the Wall the fourth tile and place it alongside his Kong to make 5 tiles, he has the right to withdraw the Loose Tile from his set and place it back in his hand to be used again. There is no set of 5 tiles in Mah Jong.

PART III

METHOD OF PLAY

METHOD OF PLAY

As explained previously, the hands are dealt out first, East Wind always being the first to discard a tile he does not require face upwards on the table. This tile may be claimed by another player to form a Pung, Kong, Mah Jong, or for a Chow (from the player on the right of East Wind). If no player claims this tile it becomes a Dead Tile and South Wind then proceeds to pick up a tile from the Wall and discards a tile he does not require, followed by West Wind and then North, and so on. This procedure goes on in an anticlockwise direction until one of the players claims a tile for a Pung or Kong. A tile to form a Pung or Kong may be claimed at any time, irrespective of turn of play by any player. The player who claims the tile for a Pung or Kong declares it on the table in front of him, discarding a tile he does not require and the next player in rotation continues the game by drawing a tile and discarding.

Thus it will be found that one or two players may miss a turn, e.g. East Wind has discarded a Red Dragon and North Wind pungs it. Actually, after East Wind discards the Dragon it was South Wind's turn to draw from the Wall, but North Wind having punged, South and West Winds both lose their turns as East Wind is next in rotation from the person who punged.

As soon as any player has completed his hand with four sets and one Pair, or any of the Special Hands, he announces Mah Jong, places all his tiles face up on the table and proceeds to count up his hand – the ground score being ascertained first and then the number of doubles. The other players likewise place their uncompleted hands face upwards on the table and ascertain their scores in the same manner. When each player has been paid his total score, the tiles are all thrown into the centre of the table, shuffled, and the Wall is built again. Then the same procedure takes place again.

A player may find that during the playing of a hand some of the tiles he requires are dead and he cannot complete the hand. In this case he has to change his hand to the best advantage according to the tiles he draws from the Wall, e.g. a player may be going for a Wriggling Snake and suddenly finds there are four North Winds discarded on the table; he cannot complete the Wriggly. The hand must be changed, and this type of hand very often develops into Concealed Mah Jong as the run from one to nine can be broken up into Chows.

Also, a Unique Wonder often develops into an All Honour Hand by forming the Pairs first and then Punging and Konging.

N.B. A player must be careful to watch the discards in case he finds himself Fishing for a Dead Tile.

PLAYERS REQUIRING THE SAME TILE

1. It often happens that two, and sometimes three players require the same tile, one for a Pung or Kong, one for a Chow and one to complete his hand for Mah Jong. In this case the player who wants it for Mah Jong has a prior right to it. Also two players may require the same tile for Mah Jong, one for a Pung and one for a Chow. The player with a Pung has precedence over the one with a Chow; in all other cases of players requiring the same tile for Mah Jong, the player next in rotation from the discarder claims it, e.g. South Wind discards a tile and West and North Winds both want it for Mah Jong. West Wind being next in rotation claims it only, and not the one who calls out first; but if North Wind had wanted it for a Pung and West for a Chow, North Wind would get it.

2. Two players may require the same tile – one for a Pung and one for a Chow. The player for a Pung claims it only, as a Pung take preference over a Chow.

Remember: a player who goes Mah Jong has preference over everything.

EAST WIND

The player who starts each game is known as East Wind. It must be borne in mind that East Wind pays and receives double. In other words, he pays the other players double their scores and receives double his score from the other players. Should East Wind go Mah Jong he remains East Wind again for the next hand, or hands, until another player goes Mah Jong, when the person who was South Wind for that hand becomes the new East Wind. West Wind becomes South, North becomes West and East becomes North. In other words East Wind does not remain stationary unless he goes Mah Jong.

WIND OF THE ROUND

There is always a Wind of the Round known as Prevailing Wind. This means that if a player has a Pung or a Kong of the Prevailing Wind he receives a double for it, also the Wind of the Round may be a player's own Wind as well, in which case he receives two doubles for the one Pung or Kong, i.e. one double for his own Wind and one double for the Wind of the Round.

The first Wind of the Round is East, the second being South, the third West, and the fourth North. When the player who was the original East Wind becomes East Wind again, that is, when the other three players have been East Wind, the Wind of the Round changes to the South, and so on.

METHODS OF COUNTING

The player who goes Mah Jong is the first to count up his ground score, counting Pungs, Kongs, Flowers and any other points (see scoring). Then he adds 20 points to his score for going Mah Jong, thus ascertaining the ground score. Only the Mah Jong hand adds 20 points. This being done, he proceeds to find the total number of doubles contained in his hand (see Scoring and Doubling lists). He then doubles his ground score for the number of doubles contained in his hand and is paid by each of the other three players. The player who goes Mah Jong does not have to pay the other players for their hands. That is the object of going Mah Jong – to avoid paying out, but to receive payment from the other players.

The other players ascertain in the same manner their total scores and pay each other in turn – East Wind paying double and receiving double for his own score. Payment is made by means of chips or counters provided with each set. Usually these chips are marked in three or four different ways in each set, by small dots – some in red and some in black and red dots. There is no set rule as to which is which, but players can call the chips what they like.

100's, 500's, 1000's are usually the recognised ones, and sometimes a few are known as 2000 or 4000 chips. It is usual for each player to start with a pool of anything from 10,000 to 20,000 chips, but each player must start with the same number, for example:

It is usual to pay to the nearest 100. Anything over 50 counts to the next 100, and anything under 50 to the 100 below, e.g. 560 would count as 600; 540 would count as 500.

10	100 chips	1000
8	500 chips	4000
7	1000 chips	7000
2	4000 chips	8000
	TOTAL	20,000

To avoid paying enormous scores, a Limit must be decided on. Usually the Limit is 1000 points. East Wind receiving 2000 points and paying 2000 points to the other players for their Limit, e.g. South Wind goes Mah Jong and finds his total score is 1200, therefore, he is over the Limit and receives 1000 only from the West and North Wind and 2000 from East Wind.

Double Limits for certain hands are paid, i.e. 2000 and 4000 (see Scoring List).

Certain hands (explained later) are known as non-scoring hands, e.g. they have no scoring value and receive a bonus of 10 points. This applies only to Mah Jong Hands and Fishing Hands. A hand may be composed of four Chows, which are of no value and a Pair, which scores 2 points, therefore this hand is a scoring hand.

GOULASH

When the Great Wall of China has been completely used up, and none of the four players have gone Mah Jong, the players' hands are thrown in among the Dead Tiles on the table, and the game is known as a Dead Hand. No scores are counted and the players then proceed to shuffle the tiles in the usual way, building their

Walls and proceeding to deal out a new hand in the ordinary way and a Goulash is then played.

Each player puts 100 or 200, or anything they like, into a pool and the winner or player who goes Mah Jong for that Goulash takes the pool. All hands in a Goulash are scored in the usual manner.

The player who was East Wind for that Dead Hand remains East Wind again for the Goulash, but whether he goes Mah Jong or not for the Goulash, he does not remain East Wind for the next hand, the East Wind thus passing on to the next player.

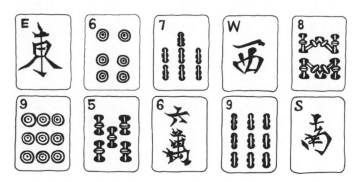

When the players have sorted their hands for the Goulash, each player picks out three tiles he does not require and exchanges these for three others with the player opposite him. Thus for the first exchange, East Wind exchanges with West Wind and South Wind with North Wind, and lastly East Wind exchanges with North and West and South Wind. This means that each player has exchanged three times. East Wind then discards a tile face up on the table and play proceeds in the usual manner.

No Chows are allowed in a Goulash, except – Imperial Jade Hand and Concealed Mah Jong (explained later).

If desired in a Goulash, the four 2's of Bamboos can be made into Jokers or Loose Tiles and may represent any tile a player needs for his hand. Therefore it is possible to have two Pungs of the same tile in the one hand, e.g. four Green Dragons and two Loose Tiles, i.e. two of the 2's of Bamboos would mean two Pungs of Green Dragons. Once a Loose Tile has been used and declared, it cannot be redeemed when a player picks up the actual tile it represents in the Pung. This tile is placed alongside the Pung already formed which makes it into a Kong.

In every Mah Jong set there are four spare tiles with no markings on them. Some players mark these with an "L" and use them instead of the 2's of Bamboos for Jokers. If this method is used then the four Jokers are used not only in a Goulash but for every hand that is played. In fact, a method has been adopted by many players whereby Goulashes are played the whole time. This must be decided upon before commencement of play. Actually, this way of playing Goulashes for every hand is not so interesting and tends to make the game too easy.

PART IV

TYPES OF HANDS

TYPES OF HANDS

Before describing these hands, there are three important things to remember.

1. The three suits **cannot** be mixed in a complete Mah Jong Hand, except four special hands:

   Triple Knitting, All Honour Hand, Unique Wonder and Concealed Mixed Pung Hand.

   Mah Jong Hands must be "cleared", i.e. one suit only, but may contain Winds and Dragons.

   A rule exists among some players that unless a hand is cleared a player may not score anything at all. This is not strictly correct. Once a Pung or Kong has been formed, it immediately has scoring value irrespective of what else is contained in the hand, and must be scored. Of course a player cannot be Fishing or go Mah Jong until he is cleared.

2. **Only one Chow is permitted** in any complete Mah Jong Hand (except the Concealed Mah Jong and Windy Chows).

3. **Fishing Hands:** A hand is said to be Fishing when a player is waiting for one tile to complete his hand. He scores this hand in exactly the same manner as if he had gone Mah Jong, except that the bonus of 20 points is not added (Scores for the Special Hands which are Fishing are given later).

   Among some players a rule exists whereby a hand scores the double for being cleared and three doubles for being cleared **with purity** when the player is not Fishing. This is not correct. Players have to be cleared before they can go Mah Jong, and are not entitled to the doubles unless they are Fishing or have gone Mah Jong. The doubles are given for going Mah Jong and for Fishing for

Mah Jong and not for being cleared. Of course Pungs and Kongs of Dragons, the Owner's Wind and the Wind of the Round and Flowers always score their doubles. Therefore a player who is not Fishing scores any Pungs and/or Kongs and takes the necessary doubles for Winds, Dragons and Flowers only.

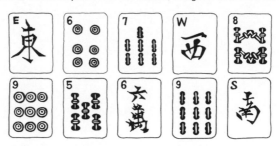

SPECIAL NOTE

Fishing Hands can now be scored in two different ways. Players may choose the way they prefer best, but this must be done prior to commencement of play. The new method of scoring Fishing Hands is:

Half Limit Hands score 200 and 400 to and from East Wind.
Limit Hands score 400 and 800 to and from East Wind.
Double Limit Hands score 500 and 1000 to and from East Wind.

Therefore it is not necessary to add up the hands and estimate the number of doubles. A set score is paid with the exception of the Ordinary Suit Hand, Purity, Concealed Mah Jong and All Honour Hand. These hands are scored in the usual way.

1 | ORDINARY SUIT HANDS

This is composed of Pungs and/or Kongs of one suit only, with Winds and/or Dragons, one Chow, (if desired) and a Pair.

SCORE:

1 double for going Mah Jong with a cleared suit and Dragons and/or Winds plus any other doubles for Dragons, Owner's and/or Wind of the Round, Owner's Flower and if all Pungs.

FISHING:

The same number of doubles as above without the bonus of 20.

2 | PURITY HANDS

In this hand there are no Winds and Dragons, it is composed of Pungs and/or Kongs and one Chow (if desired) and a Pair of one suit only.

SCORE:

Three doubles for going Mah Jong, plus any extra doubles for Owner's Flowers and if all Pungs.

FISHING:

Same doubles as above without the bonus of 20.

3 | ALL KONG HANDS

This hand contains four Kongs in one suit and/or Winds and/or Dragons and a Pair.

SCORE:

A Limit for going Mah Jong.

FISHING:

The score is doubled three times for Fishing for an all Kong Hand plus any extra doubles for Winds, Dragons and Flowers, and if All Purity, an extra three doubles, or 400 and 800 to or from East Wind.

4 | CONCEALED MAH JONG OR "BURIED TREASURE"

In this hand every tile must be drawn from the Wall including the 14th tile which makes Mah Jong. At **no time** can any tile be taken from a discard to form this hand. There can be no Kongs in this hand as Kongs have to be declared on the table. The hand must be entirely concealed.

This hand is made up of one suit only with Winds and/or Dragons and Pair, or it can be a Purity Hand No. 2, or an All Honour Hand No. 6 as well. Also as many Chows as desired are permitted. Should this hand be composed of four Chows and a non-scoring Pair it is known as a non-scoring hand and receives a bonus of 10 points for Fishing Hands and the same for Mah Jong Hands.

SCORE:

Two doubles for Concealed Mah Jong plus one double for going Mah Jong, with one suit and Winds and/or Dragons or three doubles for Purity or all Honours, plus any other doubles for Dragons, Winds, Flowers and if all Pungs.

FISHING:

The same number of doubles as above without the bonus of 20 points are scored, provided the hand contains two Chows or more. By having two or more Chows this makes the hand a definitely concealed hand, as only one Chow is permitted in an exposed hand.

If this Fishing Hand happens to contain only one Chow or none at all, the two doubles given for Fishing for a concealed hand are not permitted, as this hand, not being completed as a concealed hand, could be an Ordinary Suit Hand by going Mah Jong with a discard.

Actually, the Fishing Hand containing one Chow or none at all, all concealed, has two chances of going Mah Jong – either by completing the hand from a discard, making it an Ordinary Suit Hand exposed, or by completing the hand by drawing tiles from the Wall, making it a concealed hand.

5 | MIXED PUNG HAND (CONCEALED ONLY)

This is composed of four Pungs and a Pair in any of the three suits and may contain Winds and/or Dragons if desired. This is an exception when the three suits may be mixed, but **every tile must be drawn from the Wall including the 14th tile for Mah Jong**.

No discards can be claimed to form any of the Concealed Pungs or the Pair.

SCORE:

A Limit.

FISHING:

The Pungs are scored as Exposed Pungs, plus Flowers, and doubled three times for Fishing for Concealed Mixed Pungs, plus any doubles for Dragons, Winds and Flowers, or 400 and 800 to or from East Wind.

6 | ALL HONOUR HAND

This hand is composed of Pungs and/or Kongs of 1's and/or 9's of any of the three suits with Winds and/or Dragons and a Pair of any of the Honours.

SCORE:

Three doubles for going Mah Jong with an All Honour Hand (this includes the doubles for all Pungs), plus any other doubles for Dragons, Winds and Flowers; also if the 1's and/or 9's are one suit only an extra double for cleared suit is scored.

FISHING:

The same doubles as above without the bonus of 20.

N.B. Some players insist that this hand is incomplete unless it contains 1's **and** 9's. This is not strictly correct. The hand may contain 1's only or 9's only with Dragons and/or Winds. The only necessary tiles are All Honours Mixed.

7 | CHINESE ODDS

4 Pungs and/or Kongs of the odd numbers all in one suit (i.e. 1, 3, 5, 7, 9) and a Pair of odd numbers.

SCORE:
A Limit.

FISHING:
The ground score is doubled 3 times plus any doubles for Flowers or 400 and 800.

8 | WRIGGLY OR THE "WRIGGLING SNAKE"

This hand is composed of one suit only and must contain a run of the tiles numbered 1 to 9, one of each of the Winds and any of these thirteen tiles must be paired to complete the hand. All the tiles must be drawn from the Wall except the last tile to complete the hand and this may be taken from a discard.

SCORE:
A Limit.

FISHING:
This being a non-scoring hand the player who is Fishing for it scores 10 points, plus 4 each for any Flowers and doubles the score three times for Fishing for a Wriggly, plus extra doubles for Flowers, or 400 and 800 to or from East Wind.

9 | SPARROWS' SANCTUARY

2 Pairs of the 1's of Bamboos (Sparrows).

1 Pair of each of the green Bamboos (2, 3, 4, 6 and 8).

All tiles must be taken from the Wall except the last tile, which may be taken from a discard.

SCORE:
A Limit.

FISHING:
10 points for a non-scoring hand plus 4 for each Flower and the total score is doubled 3 times plus any double for Flowers or 400 and 800.

10 | DRAGONFLY

One of each of the Dragons.

A Pung and/or Kong of each of the 3 suits (i.e. Circles, Characters and Bamboos).

A Pair of any suit.

SCORE:
A Limit if all tiles are taken from the Wall except the last, which may be taken from a discard. If the Pungs are taken from a discard, the score is a Half Limit.

FISHING:

The ground score is doubled 3 times plus any doubles for Flowers or 400 and 800.

11 | KNITTING

This hand is made up of seven Pairs of tiles in two suits only, with no Winds and Dragons, and must be formed by drawing all the tiles from the Wall except the last tile to make Mah Jong, which may be taken from a discard. To form this hand two suits are chosen and one tile of one suit must be paired with the corresponding tile of the other suit and so on until the hand is completed.

SCORE:
A Half Limit.

FISHING:
Being a non-scoring hand, a bonus of 10 points is given to a player who is Fishing for Knitting plus 4 each for Flowers, and doubles his score twice for Fishing, plus any extra doubles for Flowers, or 200 and 400 to or from East Wind.

12 | TRIPLE KNITTING

This hand is composed of four sets of three tiles and a Pair, and is obtained in the same manner as the ordinary Knitting Hand except that each set of three tiles must have one of **each suit of the same number**, e.g. the 2 of Bamboos, 2 of Characters, 2 of Circles (one set), and so on. The Pair must be an ordinary Knitting Pair.

SCORE:
A Half Limit.

FISHING:
This is a non-scoring hand, so a player scores 10 points for Fishing, plus 4 of each Flower and doubles the score twice, plus extra doubles for Flowers, or 200 and 400 to or from East Wind.

N.B. This is a very simple hand and is omitted among some players.

13 ALL PAIR HANDS

This is made up of all Pairs in one suit with Winds and/or Dragons, every tile being drawn from the Wall except the last, which can be taken from a discard.

SCORE:
A Half Limit.

FISHING:
10 points for a non-scoring hand is given, plus 4 for each Flower, and the score is doubled twice plus extra doubles for Flowers, or 200 and 400 to or from East Wind.

N.B. No Mixed Pair hands are allowed except, of course, Knitting and All Honour Hands.

14 | ALL PAIR HONOUR HANDS

The same rule applies to this hand as in No. 13, except that the Pairs are made up of 1's and/or 9's of any of the three suits mixed with Winds and/or Dragons. This may also contain 1's and 9's only, or Winds and Dragons only.

SCORE:
A Limit.

FISHING:
10 points for a non-scoring hand plus 4 for each Flower and the score is doubled three times plus extra doubles for Flowers, or 400 and 800 to or from East Wind.

15 | ALL PAIR JADE HAND

This is made up of all Pairs of the Green Bamboo Tiles only, i.e. 2's, 3's, 4's, 6's and 8's, plus the Green Dragons. There must be a Pair of Green Dragons – it is not a Jade Hand without them.

SCORE:
A Limit.

FISHING:
10 points for a non-scoring hand plus 4 for each Flower and the score is doubled three times, plus extra doubles for Flowers, or 400 and 800 to or from East Wind.

16 ALL PAIR RUBY JADE HAND

This is made up of all Pairs of the Red and Green Bamboo Tiles, i.e. all inclusive – 1's to 9's, plus the Red and Green Dragons. There must be a Pair of each of the Red and Green Dragon's – it is not a Ruby Jade Hand without them.

SCORE:
A Limit.

FISHING:
10 points for a non-scoring hand plus 4 of each Flower and the score is doubled three times, plus extra doubles for the Flowers, or 400 and 800 to or from East Wind.

17 HEAVENLY TWINS

This hand is made up of seven Pairs of tiles all in the one suit with no Winds and Dragons. Every tile must be drawn from the Wall except the last to make Mah Jong, which may be taken from a discard.

SCORE:
A Limit.

FISHING:
10 points for a non-scoring hand plus three doubles for Fishing for Heavenly Twins, plus extra doubles for Flowers, or 400 and 800 to or from East Wind.

Pung or Kong of Red Dragons.

Pung or Kong of White Dragons.

Pung or Kong of Green Dragons.

Pung or Kong of own Wind when it is also the Wind of the Round.

Pair of any Wind.

A Bouquet of Flowers must also be held.

SCORE:

All players must pay out their complete pool of counters in hand, whatever they may be, to the winner, who has therefore won the table. The other players then pay in cash the value of their original pool to the winner and the counters are then divided up in that pool again and a fresh start is made.

This is an extremely difficult hand to get and any player lucky enough to get it deserves to win all the counters.
It may be said that this hand is impossible to get, but nothing is impossible if luck is on your side.

TYPES OF HANDS

FISHING:

A Limit.

N.B. This hand can only be obtained when the Pung of Winds is the owner's double-double, i.e. East Wind can only obtain this hand when it is East Wind's round, South Wind can only get it when it is South Wind's round and so on.

19 UNIQUE WONDER OR "THIRTEEN GRADES OF IMPERIAL TREASURE"

This hand is made up of one each of the 1's and 9's of each suit, one of each of the Winds and one of each of the Dragons. Any of the thirteen tiles mentioned must be paired to go Mah Jong. All these tiles must be picked up off the Wall except the 14th tile to complete Mah Jong which may be taken from a discard.

SCORE:

A Double Limit, i.e. 2000 points and 4000 for East Wind.

FISHING:

10 points for a non-scoring hand plus 4 for each Flower and the score is doubled three times, plus any extra doubles for Flowers, or 500 and 1000 to or from East Wind.

20 LILY OF THE VALLEY

Pung or Kong of White Dragons.

Pung or Kong of Green Dragons.

2 Pungs or Kongs of any of the Green Bamboos (2, 3, 4, 6 and 8).

1 Pair of Green Bamboos.

All tiles may be Punged from a discard.

SCORE:
Double Limit.

FISHING:
Pungs and Kongs are counted as usual plus points for any Flowers and the total score is doubled 3 times, plus any doubles for Flowers and Dragons or 500 and 1000.

21 IMPERIAL JADE HAND

All tiles in this hand must be Green, therefore the Bamboo Suit and the Green Dragons are used. The hand is made up in the same way as an Ordinary Suit Hand of Pungs and/or Kongs and one Chow, if so desired.

Only the 2's, 3's, 4's, 6's, and 8's are green.

The Jade Hand must contain a Pung or Kong of the Green Dragons. It is not an Imperial Jade Hand without them.

SCORE:

A Double Limit.

FISHING:

The ground score is doubled three times for Fishing for the Imperial Jade Hand plus any extra doubles for Flowers, Green Dragons and if all Pungs, or 500 and 1000 to and from East Wind.

N.B. This is a very difficult hand to get when playing with experienced players. As soon as a player has made one or two Exposed Pungs or Kongs of the Green Tiles, the other players immediately suspect this hand to be an Imperial Jade Hand, and endeavour to block this player from going Mah Jong by keeping all the Green Tiles concealed in their hands. Therefore it is very dangerous to make a Kong with the Green Tiles. A player going for a Jade Hand can therefore bluff the other players by letting the Kongs go by. If he has a Concealed Pung of Green Tiles in his hand and picks up a fourth making a Kong, he should discard it, thereby leaving a doubt in the other players' minds as to whether or not he is going for a Jade Hand. Of course once a Pung is made and declared on the table it does not matter about making it into a Kong, but beware of the 2's, 3's, and 4's of Bamboos – make quite sure you do not need a Chow before Konging any of these. Keep as much as possible concealed in the hand.

22 | ROYAL RUBY HAND

This hand is similar to the Jade Hand and is composed of Pungs and/or Kongs and a Pair of Bamboo Suit again, using the 1's, 5's, 7's and 9's and the Red Dragons, therefore no Chows can be obtained. It is **absolutely necessary to have the Red Dragons** as there are not enough tiles to form this hand without them.

SCORE:
A Double Limit.

FISHING:
The ground score is doubled three times plus extra doubles for Red Dragons and Flowers, or 500 and 1000 to or from East Wind.

N.B. Beware of Kongs in this hand also. It is far better to keep a Pung concealed in the hand than to make a Kong of it and expose it. Kongs make no difference to the score as it is a Double Limit in any case. This is the most difficult hand of all to get.

23 | WINDY DRAGONS

This hand contains two Pungs (not Kongs) of any of the three sets of Dragons and one Pair of each of the Winds. The Dragons may be Punged from a discard, but the four Pairs of Winds must be picked up from the Wall. The last tile to complete the hand may be taken from a discard.

SCORE:
A Limit.

FISHING:

The score of the Dragons and any scoring Pair of Winds, plus 4 for any Flowers, and the total is doubled three times plus extra doubles for Dragons or Flowers, or 400 and 800 to or from East Wind.

24 | WINDY ONES

Pungs or Kongs of each of the 1's of each suit.

One of each of the Winds.

Any of the Winds may be paired to complete the hand.

SCORE:

A Limit, provided all the Pungs are concealed in the hand, the last tile may be taken from a discard.

If the tiles are taken from a discard to form the Pungs, a Half Limit is scored.

FISHING:

The Pungs are scored as Concealed Pungs (8 points), plus any points for Flowers, and the total score is doubled 3 times plus any doubles for Flowers or 400 and 800.

25 | WINDY NINES

This is the same type of hand as Windy Ones but contains the 9's instead of the 1's.

SCORE:
The same as for Windy Ones.

FISHING:
The Pungs are scored as Concealed Pungs (8 points), plus any points for Flowers, and the total score is doubled 3 times plus any doubles for Flowers or 400 and 800.

26 SPECIAL CHINESE HAND OR THE "GATES OF HEAVEN"

One suit again is used with no Winds and Dragons and all tiles must be taken from the Wall, except the last tile, which may be taken from a discard. The hand is composed of a Pung of 1's, a Pung of 9's, and one each of the tiles numbered 2 to 8. To complete the hand with a Pair, any one of the tiles numbered 2 to 8 must be paired.

SCORE:
A Limit.

FISHING:
10 points for the non-scoring hand, 4 for each Flower, and the total is doubled three times for Fishing plus any doubles for Flowers, or 400 and 800 to or from East Wind.

27 A RUN, PUNG AND A PAIR

This hand is composed of one suit only with no Winds and Dragons. It contains the complete run from 1 to 9, a Pung and a Pair, all in the same suit. Each tile must be taken from the Wall except the last to complete the hand, which may be taken from a discard.

SCORE:
A Limit.

FISHING:
10 points for a non-scoring hand, 4 for each Flower, and the total is doubled three times, plus extra doubles for Flowers, or 400 and 800 to or from East Wind.

28 | 1'S AND 9'S, OR HEADS AND TAILS

This hand is composed of Pungs and/or Kongs of 1's and 9's of any of the three suits, and a Pair of either 1's or 9's. There are no Winds or Dragons in this hand.

SCORE:
A Limit.

FISHING:
The ground score is doubled three times for All Honours and one extra double for all 1's and 9's, plus extra doubles for Flowers, or 400 and 800 to or from East Wind.

29 | ALL WINDS AND DRAGON HANDS

This hand is composed of Pungs and/or Kongs of Winds and Dragons only, with no suit tiles.

SCORE:
A Limit.

FISHING:
The ground score is doubled three times for All Honours, plus one extra double for all Winds and Dragons, plus extra doubles for Flowers, Dragons and Winds, or 400 and 800 to or from East Wind.

30 THREE GREAT SCHOLARS

In this hand there are three Pungs and/or Kongs of all the three Dragons plus a Pung, Kong or a Chow, and a Pair of a suit and/or Winds.

SCORE:
A Limit.

FISHING:
A Limit is scored for any hand containing the Three Great Scholars, whether Fishing or not.

N.B. Beware of Konging the Dragons in this hand also.

31 THE FOUR BLESSINGS

This hand contains Pungs and/or Kongs of each of the Four Winds and a Pair of anything.

SCORE:
A Limit.

FISHING:
A Limit is scored, whether Fishing or not, if the hand contains the four complete sets of Winds.

N.B. Beware of Konging the Winds.

32 HEAVEN'S GRACE

If East Wind picks up his original fourteen tiles, and finds this hand completed, irrespective of his scoring value or cleared suit he has a Heaven's Grace. Only East Wind can pick up a completed Mah Jong Hand having fourteen tiles to start with and declare it immediately.

SCORE:
A Double Limit.

33 EARTH'S GRACE

This is scored by any player who, on picking up his original thirteen tiles, finds that he is Fishing for Mah Jong straight away, and on the first discard made by East Wind, completes his hand.

SCORE:
A Limit.

34 RED LANTERN

Pung or Kong of Red Dragons.

Pung or Kong of Own Wind.

Run from 1 to 7 in same suit.

Any tile from 1 to 7 may form the Pair.

SCORE:
Double Limit, provided all tiles are taken from a discard. If the Pungs are made from a discard, the score is a Limit.

FISHING:
The ground score, i.e. points for the sets of Winds and Dragons and Flowers, is doubled 3 times plus double for any Flowers and the Winds and Dragons, or 500 and 1000.

35 RED LILY

Pung or Kong of White Dragons.

2 Pungs and/or Kongs of Red Bamboos (i.e. 1, 5, 7, 9).

Pung or Kong of Red Dragons.

A Pair of Red Bamboos.

SCORE:
Double Limit

FISHING:
Ground score is doubled 3 times, plus double for Dragons and any Flowers, or 500 and 1000.

---

36 | PLUCKING THE PLUM BLOSSOM FROM THE ROOF

The 5 of Circles is shown as the Plum Blossom. To obtain this hand a player must be Fishing for the 5 of Circles to complete this hand. If he should make a Kong or pick up a Flower, he takes one of the Loose Tiles to replace the Flower or Kong, and should this Loose Tile be the 5 of Circles and he goes Mah Jong with it, he has plucked the Plum Blossom from the Roof.

SCORE:
A Limit, irrespective of the value of his hand.

---

37 | PICKING THE MOON FROM THE BOTTOM OF THE SEA

The 1 of Circles is known as The Moon of China. A player must be calling for the 1 of Circles to complete his hand for Mah Jong and should he pick up this 1 of Circles to complete the hand himself, when it is the last tile left on the Wall, he has then Picked the Moon from the Bottom of the Sea.

SCORE:
A Limit, irrespective of the value of his hand.

38 | RUBY JADE

This hand is partly the Imperial Jade Hand and partly the Royal Ruby Hand. It is composed of a Pung or Kongs of Red Dragons, a Pung of Green Dragons, a Pung of Green Bamboo Tiles (2's, 3's, 4's, 6's or 8's) and a Pung of the remaining Bamboo Tiles (1's, 5's, 7's or 9's), and the Pair may be any Pair of the Bamboo Suit.

SCORE:
A Limit.

FISHING:
The ground score is doubled 3 times, plus extra doubles for Flowers and Dragons, or 400 and 800 to or from East Wind.

39 | WINDY CHOWS

This hand contains one of each of the Winds, one Chow in the Character Suit, one Chow in the Circle Suit, one Chow in the Bamboo Suit and any of the Winds must be paired.

SCORE:
Half Limit.

FISHING:
10 points are scored for a non-scoring hand, plus 4 points for any Flowers, and a score is doubled twice, or 200 and 400 to or from East Wind.

40 | GERTIE'S GARTER

This hand is actually an ordinary Knitting Hand, but the seven Pairs must start at No. 1 and end with No. 7. Therefore Pairs of 8's and 9's are not permitted.

SCORE:
A Limit.

FISHING:
10 points are scored for a non-scoring hand, plus three doubles for Fishing, plus any double for Flowers, or 400 and 800 to or from East Wind.

41 | GRETA'S GARDEN

This hand is composed of one of each of the Dragons, one of each of the Winds and a run from 1 to 7, all in the one suit. This hand does not contain a Pair and is the one exception to the rule.

SCORE:
A Limit.

FISHING:

10 points are scored for a non-scoring hand, plus three doubles for Fishing, plus doubles for any Flowers, or 400 and 800 to or from East Wind.

SPECIAL RULES

1. ROBBING THE KONG

A player may be waiting for a certain tile to complete his hand and finds that another player has an Exposed Pung of this tile on the table, leaving one more on the Wall. If the player with the Exposed Pung of the tile required by another player, should pick up the fourth one and place it alongside his Pung to make it into an Exposed Kong, the player who requires that fourth tile to complete his hand may claim it, thereby robbing the Kong. A Concealed Kong **cannot** be robbed.

SCORE: 1 extra double for Robbing the Kong.

2. GOING MAH JONG WITH A LOOSE TILE

If a player is waiting for a certain tile to complete his hand and he draws a Loose Tile from the Wall, for a Flower or Kong, and at the same time this tile completes his hand for Mah Jong, he has gone Mah Jong with a Loose Tile.

SCORE: 1 extra double.

3. RE-SHUFFLE

Should any player, on picking up his original hand, find that he has no Winds or Dragons, 1's or 9's, Flowers, and no Pungs, Kongs, Chows or Pairs, he may claim a re-shuffle. This means that the other three players must throw their hands in also.

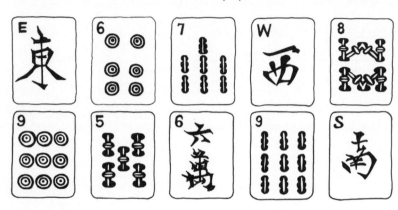

PENALTIES

1. A PLAYER HOLDING TOO FEW TILES

Should any player during the game find himself with too few tiles he cannot correct this error. He may score his hand, but of course, cannot go Mah Jong.

2. A PLAYER HOLDING TOO MANY TILES

Should a player find himself with too many tiles, he also is not permitted to correct this error, and cannot score his hand at all. Also he cannot go Mah Jong.

3. DECLARING A FALSE MAH JONG

A player may declare Mah Jong and on exposing his hand, suddenly find that he is not Mah Jong. If in the meantime the other players have exposed their hands, the player who has declared the false Mah Jong must pay a penalty of a Half Limit to each of the other players.

SPECIAL NOTES

1. The worst conceivable sin in Mah Jong is to be a slow player. Try and make your pick-ups and discards quickly. Do not keep the other players waiting for their turn.
2. Carefully watch what has been discarded otherwise you may be requiring a tile of which there are four dead on the table.
3. When players start to draw tiles from your Wall, push it in towards the centre so that they can be picked up easily.
4. As players become experts there is ample scope to bluff opponents as in Poker – never permit other players to see that you hold a good hand.
5. Watch the tiles the other players are discarding and try to ascertain the type of hand they are acquiring. With experience you will be able to tell more or less what they are going for and what tiles they require.
6. If you think another player is going for a Limit or a Double Limit Hand, and you have a very poor hand, even though you may go Mah Jong, it will pay you to break up your hand, keeping dangerous tiles concealed and discarding safe tiles.

SCORING

The easiest method of scoring is to remember that Concealed Pungs and Kongs are worth twice the value of Exposed Pungs and Kongs. Also Pungs and Kongs of Winds and Dragons, 1's and 9's are worth double the value of all suit tiles numbered 2 to 8.

All Kongs are worth four times the value of the same tiles when they are a Pung.

	EXPOSED ON THE TABLE	CONCEALED IN THE HAND
Pungs of tiles numbered 2 to 8	2	4
Pungs of 1s, 9s, Winds and Dragons	4	8
Kongs of tiles numbered 2 to 8	8	16
Kongs of 1s, 9s, Winds and Dragons	16	32

All Chows count 0.

The Player who goes Mah Jong adds 20 to his score.

EXTRA POINTS

In the following cases 2 points are added to the player's score:

1. Any Pair of Dragons.
2. Pair of Owner's Wind.
3. Pair of the Wind of the Round.

4. By going Mah Jong in the only possible place – in the middle of a Chow or at the end of a Chow, e.g. with a 3 or a 7.

5. By drawing a tile from the Wall to make Mah Jong.

6. By completing the Sparrow's Head, e.g. by completing the Pair for Mah Jong.

7. For Punging or Konging the 1st discard made by East Wind.

All Flowers count 4 points.

A hand which is made up of Four Chows and a non-scoring Pair (Concealed Mah Jong only) is called a non-scoring hand and scores 10 points.

DOUBLES

(A) 1 DOUBLE:

These sets of tiles all double the score once:

1. All one suit with Winds and Dragons.
2. All Pungs.
3. Each Pung or Kong of Dragons.
4. Pung or Kong of Owner's Wind.
5. Pung or Kong of Wind of the Round.
6. Each of the Owner's Flowers.
7. By going Mah Jong with a Loose Tile off the Wall.
8. By going Mah Jong with the last tile off Wall when it is the last tile to be picked up.
9. By robbing the Kong.

(B) 2 DOUBLES:

The following hand doubles the score twice – Concealed Mah Jong Hand or Buried Treasure, plus extra doubles for one suit, Winds, Dragons, Flowers and if all Pungs.

(C) 3 DOUBLES:

The following sets of tiles double the score three times:

1. Purity Hand plus extra doubles for Flowers and if all Pungs.
2. Bouquet of Flowers.
3. All Honour Hand plus extra doubles for Winds, Dragons or Flowers.

(D) HALF LIMIT HANDS:

1. Knitting.
2. Triple Knitting.
3. All Pair Hand.
4. Windy Chows.
5. Windy Ones (if Pungs are formed from discards).
6. Windy Nines (same as Windy Ones).

(E) LIMIT HANDS:

1. Run, Pung and a Pair.
2. Heavenly Twins.
3. Wriggling Snake.
4. All Pair Honour Hand.

5. Special Chinese Hand or the Gates of Heaven.

6. Hand composed of Pungs and Kongs of 1's to 9's only.

7. Hand composed of Pungs and Kongs of Winds and Dragons only.

8. The Three Great Scholars.

9. The Four Blessings of Pungs and Kongs of the Four Winds.

10. Windy Dragons.

11. By Plucking the Plum Blossom from the Roof.

12. By Picking the Moon from the Bottom of the Sea.

13. An all Kong hand.

14. Concealed Mixed Pung Hand.

15. Earth's Grace.

16. Ruby Jade.

17. All Pair Jade Hand.

18. All Pair Ruby Red Hand.

19. Sparrow's Sanctuary.

20. Windy Ones (provided all Pungs are concealed).

21. Windy Nines (same as Windy Ones).

22. Red Lantern (if Pungs are made from discards).

23. Chinese Odds.

24. Dragonfly (if tiles are taken from the Wall).

25. Heavenly Paradise (if Fishing for this hand).

(F) DOUBLE LIMIT:

1. Unique Wonder.
2. Imperial Jade Hand.
3. Royal Ruby Hand.
4. Heaven's Grace, i.e. when the East Wind picks up a complete Mah Jong Hand.
5. Lily of the Valley.
6. Red Lantern (provided all tiles are from the Wall).
7. Red Lily.

EXAMPLES OF SCORING

1. South Wind went Mah Jong with an Ordinary Suit Hand, when the Wind of the Round was East. He completed the hand by drawing the East Wind from the Wall to complete the Pair. The completed hand contained:

Own Flower No. 2		4 Points
1 Pung concealed – 2 Circles		4 Points
1 Kong exposed – Red Dragons		16 Points
1 Pung of South Winds exposed		4 Points
1 Kong concealed – 9 Circles		32 Points
One Pair of East Wind:	For going Mah Jong with Pair	2 Points
	Pair of Wind of Round	2 Points
	For Drawing it from Wall	2 Points
Bonus for going Mah Jong		20 Points
	GROUND SCORE TOTAL	86 Points

DOUBLES:

Kong of Red Dragons	1 double
Pung of Own Wind	1 double
Going Mah Jong with suit and Honours	1 double
For all Pungs	1 double
Own Flower	1 double
TOTAL	5 doubles

Therefore South Wind doubles his ground score of 86, five times. This gives a total of 2752, which is a Limit Hand.

West and North Winds each pay South Wind 1000 and East Wind pays 2000.

2. North Wind went Mah Jong with an All Honour Hand when it was South Wind's round. The hand contained:

1 Exposed Pung of 1's of Circles	4 Points
1 Exposed Pung of 1's of Bamboos	4 Points
1 Exposed Pung of South Winds	4 Points
1 Exposed Pung of 1's of Characters	4 Points
1 Pair of Red Dragons	2 Points
Bonus for going Mah Jong	20 Points
GROUND SCORE TOTAL	38 Points

For going Mah Jong with All Honours	3 doubles
For Pung of Wind of the Round (South)	1 double
TOTAL	4 doubles

Thus the Ground score of 38 doubled four times is 604. East Wind pays double 604, which is 1208. Therefore South and West Winds both pay 600 each and East Wind pays 1200.

3. East Wind was Fishing for an Ordinary Suit Hand when it was East Wind's round. The Hand contained:

Own Flower No.1	4 Points
1 Exposed Pung of East Winds	4 Points
1 Exposed Kong of 2's Characters	8 Points
1 Concealed Pung of 4's of Characters	4 Points
1 Pair of Green Dragons	2 Points
1 Pair of 8's of Characters	0 Points
GROUND SCORE TOTAL	22 Points

East Wind was therefore Fishing for a Green Dragon, or an 8 of Characters to complete his hand.

DOUBLES:

Fishing for an Ordinary Suit Hand	1 double
Fishing for all Pungs	1 double
Pung of Wind of the Round	1 double
Pung of Own Wind	1 double
Own Flower	1 double
TOTALS	5 doubles

Thus 22 doubled five times is 704. Therefore South and West Winds (North went Mah Jong and does not pay) must pay East Wind double his score of 704, which is 1408 (they actually pay 1400).

4. Another player had gone Mah Jong when it was South Wind's Round. South Wind was not Fishing, but his hand contained:

1 Pung exposed of South Winds	4 Points
1 Concealed Pung of Green Dragons	8 Points
1 Exposed Pung of 2's of Circles	2 Points
1 8's of Characters	0 Points
1 3's of Bamboos	0 Points
1 North Wind	0 Points
1 East Wind	0 Points
Own Flower No. 2	4 Points
TOTAL	**18 Points**

DOUBLES:

1 Pung of Wind of the Round	1 double
1 Pung of Own Wind (South)	1 double
1 Concealed Pung of Green Dragons	1 double
Own Flower	1 double
TOTALS	**4 doubles**

Therefore he doubles his ground score of 18, four times which is 288, and East Wind pays 576. Actually, he receives 300 from one player and 600 from East Wind. It will be noticed that this hand is not completely cleared, but he still scores his Pungs and Kongs.

PART VI

THE THREE- AND TWO-HANDED GAMES OF MAH JONG

THE THREE- AND TWO-HANDED GAMES OF MAH JONG

THE THREE-HANDED GAME

In the three-handed game, the players proceed in exactly the same way as in the four-handed game, but no Chows are permitted except in a Jade Hand and a Concealed Mah Jong Hand.

The scoring is exactly the same except that the double for All Pungs is omitted unless the whole hand is a Concealed Pung Hand.

As in the four-handed game, each player has a Wind of his own. Consequently there is always one vacant Wind.

GOULASH

In a three-handed game, a Goulash is played in the same manner as in the four-handed game with each player making three exchanges. As the fourth seat in this game is vacant, the player opposite this vacant seat takes three tiles anywhere from the Wall and replaces these with three from his own hand. Likewise, the other players do the same when it is their turn to change with the vacant seat.

THE TWO-HANDED GAME

This is very good practice for beginners. The two players sit opposite one another, one being East Wind and the other West Wind. The play is exactly the same as in the four-handed game except:

    (1) There are no Chows allowed and there is no exception to this rule.

    (2) A player may not go Mah Jong unless his hand contains 4 doubles or more (this does not include the doubles for Flowers) but he may have any of the hands with set scores, i.e. Half Limit, Limit, and Double Limit Hands.

In order to get a hand with 4 doubles or more, a player may have to discard Pungs and Kongs of tiles which do not give doubles, in order to obtain a Pung or a Kong which will give a double. Therefore a certain amount of shuffling about and changing is necessary. The hands are scored exactly the same way and the players pay each other (this is the only time that the player who went Mah Jong has to pay out).

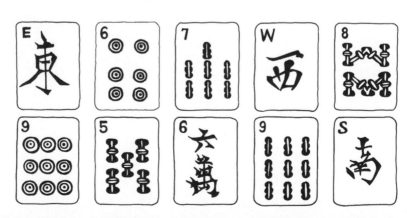

PART VII

THE CHINESE GAME

THE CHINESE GAME

Players proceed in exactly the same way as in the Western game of Mah Jong, but the Flowers are omitted.

The only hands to be obtained are hands made up of four sets (Pungs, Kongs and Chows) and a Pair, Unique Wonder, Imperial Jade and Gates of Heaven, which very rarely occur. There are none of the special hands and no all Pair hands.

The suits may be mixed and as many Chows as desired are allowed – this means that players go Mah Jong very quickly with small scores. There are very few large hands for the reason that players go Mah Jong so quickly that there is no time to form a big hand.

The Chinese play for very high stakes and that is where the excitement and thrill of the game is found.

When playing the Chinese game players draw tiles from the Wall and discard in the same manner as in the Western game, but instead of drawing all the tiles from the Wall, the Chinese leave fourteen tiles at the end of the Wall, which are not used at all. This is known as the Dead Wall (the two Loose Tiles are placed on top of the Dead Wall), therefore there are fourteen tiles which are never used, and the game becomes dead when these fourteen tiles are reached.

The scoring of the Chinese game varies a little from the Western game, the actual total score being paid.

AN EXAMPLE OF A TYPICAL CHINESE MAH JONG HAND –

South Wind's hand contained:

1 Chow of Bamboos (2, 3, 4)	0 Points
1 Pung of 3's Circles	2 Points
1 Chow of Characters (6, 7, 8)	0 Points
1 Pung of South Winds	4 Points
1 Pair Green Dragons	2 Points
Bonus for going Mah Jong	20 Points
TOTAL	**28 Points**

DOUBLES:

For Pung of own Wind = 1 double.

Thus, 28 doubled once is 56, West and North Winds both pay exactly 56 and East Wind pays 112 points.

(Doubling Table overleaf)

DOUBLING TABLE

	4	6	8	10	12	14	16	18	20	22	24
1	8	12	16	20	24	28	32	36	40	44	48
2	16	24	32	40	48	56	64	72	80	88	96
3	32	48	64	80	96	112	128	144	160	176	192
4	64	96	128	160	192	224	256	288	320	352	384
5	128	192	256	320	384	448	512	576	640	704	768
6	256	384	512	640	768	896	1024	1152	1280	1408	1536

	48	50	52	54	56	58	60	62	64	66	68
1	96	100	104	108	112	116	120	124	128	132	136
2	192	200	208	216	224	232	240	248	256	264	272
3	384	400	416	432	448	464	480	496	512	528	544
4	768	800	832	864	896	928	960	992	1024	1056	1088
5	1536	1600	1664	1728	1792	1856	1920	1984	2048	2112	2176
6	3072	3200	3328	3456	3584	3712	3840	3968	4096	4224	4352